Alive

ISBN: 9798325869020

Alive

Jacquelyn

Contents

Rise

I take off my clothes and lay
between the sheets.
I have been here before,
and I know what is being asked of me.
Energy rises in my belly,
my heart opens with my breath,
naked and raw.
I hear the whispers—
Yes, she is here, Aphrodite.
Feel her power.
Surrender to her.
My senses climb
Air enters my lungs and releases in totality,
each sensation magnified.
My hips move;
my world burns.
The beating of my heart is overcome
with the drum of my magic.
Let her have her way with you,
I hear through my heart.
My womb opens;
the water rises;
the waves crest;
their power washes over me;
my body is alive.

The rising and falling
and rising and falling—
the falling,
because there is no rising
without falling.
There is no expansion
without contraction;
no birth
without death.
The falling *is*
the rising.

The wind howls and rages,
making herself known.

The ocean crashes and recedes,
making sure she's seen.

The earth moans and releases
for all to feel.

Whatever made you think
you were meant to be tamed?

To not rage in your anger
and howl out your sadness—

to not love with all your heart
and moan out in bliss?

Who told you to be so tamed?
That's not what we are meant for;

that's not how we were made.

Play with me, invited unknown.
Dance with me, flirted curiosity.
Undress yourself, offered freedom.
Make love to me, whispered surrender.

I heard the voice
calling from my heart.
It's time, my love, it says.
It's time to face the truth,
to let yourself dream.

It's time
to let go
of unworthiness,
of shame,
of guilt,
and fear.

It's time,
my love;
it's time
to let yourself
be free.

How can you feel alive,
when you've been taught
not to feel?

Take off that shirt of fear
that covers your heart.

Slip off your pants of conformity—
they are too tight for your beautiful flesh.

Slide down your panties of shame,
their cotton woven with numbness.

Relish in your naked beauty;
touch your soul's skin feverishly,
like you've never been touched before.

Feel every crevice and delicious fold;
feel the truth of who you are
and redress yourself in sacredness.

There's always somewhere to be—
a gathering,
a career,
a lover,
a lifestyle,
a better version of yourself—

be here, instead.

What a relief
what a liberation-
to disappoint everyone as I
step out of their box.

I took a deep breath
and dropped into my body,
meeting the discomfort
that was asking to be seen.
I want to love someone,
she yearned.
I put my hands
on my heart.
Me, I said,
You have me to love.

14

Every day, I touch
the parts of me that are numb:
the places my body holds pain,
the malnourished crevices
that ache to be seen,
to be felt.
I love them
back to life.

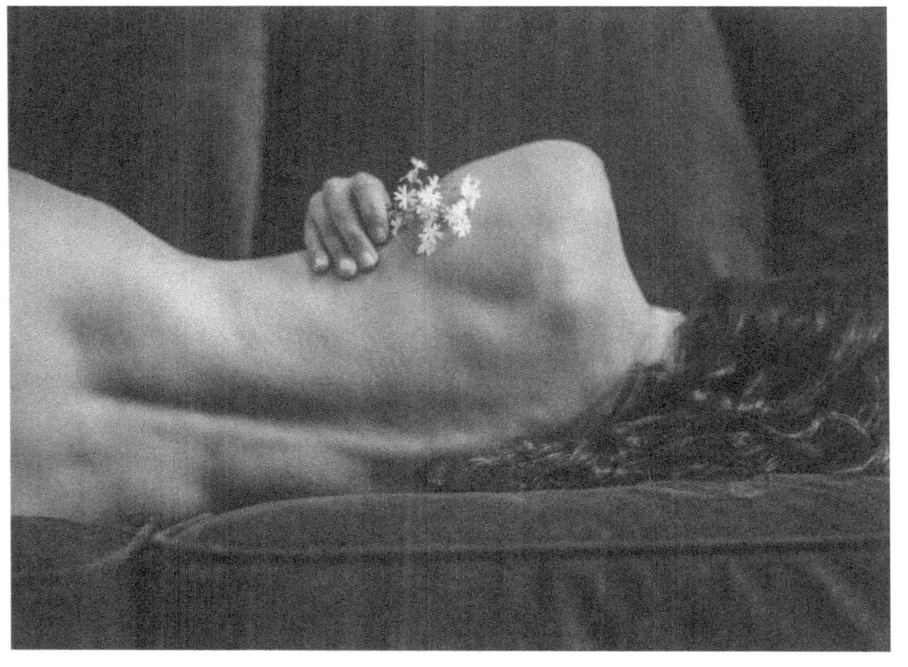

The world is speeding up-
slow down
slow down
slow down.

Can you forgive yourself?
For not being good enough?
For not doing more?
Knowing more?
Loving more?
For the choices you made out of fear?

Can you forgive yourself
for being here?

I know why you closed your heart;
I closed mine for the same reasons,
and I knew opening it again
would be painful.
But I promise
your suffering will subside,
joy will enter—
and love, oh the love.
One day you'll take a deep breath,
put your hands on your heart,
and whisper,
Thank you.

What does it feel like to be out of survival mode?
It feels like a breeze on my face,
warmth on my skin,
dew on my feet—
it feels like feeling.

I welcome the solitude,
to hold my heart and say,

I see you
I feel you
I am here.

Shed it all.
Let it burn.
Leave everything
that is keeping you from
your wild heart
and free spirit.

Make love to your fears,
caress them,
let them ravish you,
show them they are safe
to be seen and felt.

Let them move through your body,
closing your chest on the way out
as you love them to leave.

My children,
this world is designed
to take you away from yourself.

Don't let it.

Feel your body.
Keep your heart open.
Choose to stay
in the moment—
every beautiful and
terrifying moment.

You came here for this.

Listen to your inner voice,
and remember
you are in this world,
but you are not of it.

27

It's time for me to be here—
not in the stories inside of my head,
or in the fantasies I've danced with along the way—
not in the past,
not in the future,
but here.

Your body is aching for your devotion,
your touch.
Hold her and honor her,
Feel her depths.
Let her bring you to God.

You rise
the way trees rise:
unapologetically
taking up space,

strong,
rooted,
whole,

and as though you fucking belong here
because you do.

Oh, how the comfort makes it so hard.
If I can just quiet the voice inside long enough,
I might deem myself happy—
but then I catch myself dreaming,
and something stirs inside of me.
It was just a thought,
a silly one.
I should stay;
it's comfortable here.
But that voice
is too clever and too strong,
and it involved my heart.
That sneaky little voice
tells me that my comfort is a trick.

Oh, the comfort.
I don't miss you much,
for I have grown satisfied with the wild unknown.
It's much more fun here.

Take the journey back to yourself,
and then promise
to never leave her again.

It's time to bring
simplicity and sacredness
back into our lives.

35

Don't exchange your soul for likability.

My unashamed hunger
to spread my legs for the sun;
to dance naked under the open sky;   to
swim in the ocean while her depths
soak the anger from my bones;
to lay my skin on the earth's skin,
arms wide open in surrender;
to feel his mouth on every inch of my flesh;
to climb a tree and scream into the Universe;
to express my full essence.

I will not deny myself such a life
for their well-kept perception
of a good little wife.

Let me go slow.

Let me try on different hats
to see which ones I like the best.

Let me walk barefooted on the earth,
through detours and unmarked trails.

Let me start over anytime I wish.

Let me mess up.

Let me change my mind
and leave parts of me behind.

Let me sip my tea slowly
while the cars rush by,
refusing to conform
to the world outside.

I have nowhere to rush to;
I'll get there one day.

But until then,
let me go slowly,
for if there's anything I know for sure,
it's that I'll miss this earth
when I'm gone.

39

Who told you to be so put-together?
Put-together for who?
For what?

Your put-together lover?
Your put-together house?
Your put together-yard?
Your put-together life?

Who is worth all this put-togetherness?

I like my hair to portray my spirit,
wild and *unruly*.

We are all undressing,
taking off our stories,
our limiting beliefs
to put on something
a little more sacred.

We are all polishing our crowns
that have been buried
under years of conditioning,
and we are walking out
into the world,
ready to be seen.

For far too long
they have cut down our trees,
silenced our voices,
dirtied out waters,
raped our wombs,
trashed our fields,
covered our instincts,
and tamed our spirits.

But they couldn't erase us.
We rise from the ones they set aflame.
We came here for this,
this time,
this shift.
We came here for Her.
She is shaking.
She is speaking.
She is rising.

It is not my responsibility to
keep up with
your preferred version of me.

Step away from the soul dead world
of distractions and disconnection,
external fixings disguised as living,
of consuming and endless doing.

Step into the world of your heart:
live under the moon and stars,
with the trees and ocean,
with the magic of you.

She came in
untamed and alive.
I didn't know what to do with her at first.
She scared me,
intimidated me,
brought me to my knees,
and set my soul on fire.
She refused my attempts to tame her.
I refused my domestication.

Walk with me, Mama, she says.
Let me show you the way back.

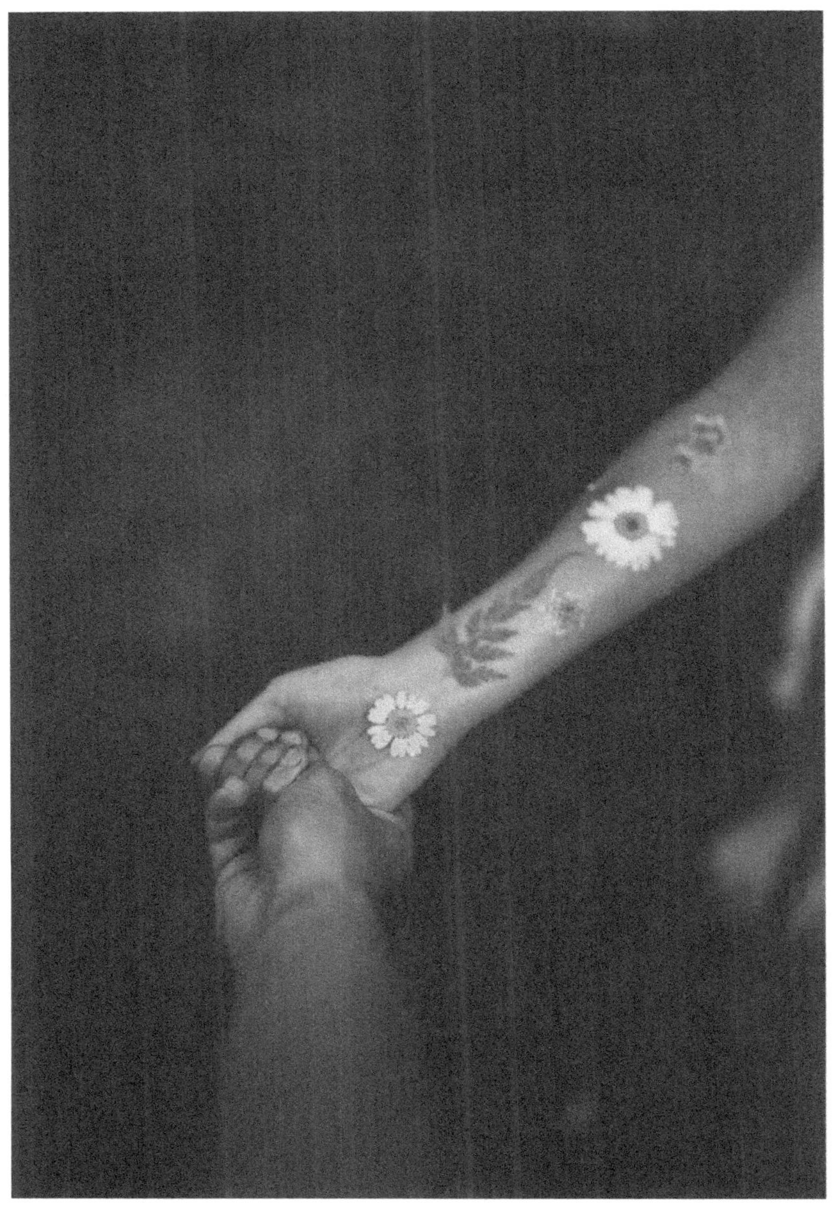

Don't let them tame you.
Don't let them give you
all their *shouldn'ts, couldn'ts,* and *mustn'ts.*

Don't step into the box they have made—
the red carpet leading to the locked exit.

Don't listen to anything
but your heart.

Don't let them tame you.

51

I refuse to play small
to accommodate your insecurities.

Your voice is connected
to your womb;
your voice should be heard
and your womb wet.
Set them both free.

53

Oh, all of these distractions
that are keeping us
from living.

I'm like the rose blooming slowly,
one petal at a time.

Each petal opens my heart,
revealing more beauty.

I take my time with myself.
I love myself open.

Don't drown yourself
just so they can see themselves
in the water's reflection.

You came here with a
passion for swimming.
You float so gracefully.

Don't deprive yourself
of all that play.

I suppose it's heartbreak
but not for anyone else—
it's for the love
I withheld from myself.

No human can love you
as much as you can love yourself.

No human that can know you
the way that you can know yourself.

They can love you with all they have—
and oh, do let them—

but don't deprive yourself
of your own sweet devotional love.

That's a love story
worth living.

Don't underestimate a woman.
It takes time to shake off the dust
of domesticity.

It takes time to realize
we have been plucked from our soul
and put in a vase on your table.

But our souls are too strong;
our hearts, too wild.
It is only a matter of time

before we rise.

We are simple,
breathing,
feeling,
thinking,
human beings.
A spirit
inside a body—
that is magic enough.

Your love and light
will only get you so far.
It's your flesh and darkness
that will let you
explode into who you are.

I feel it inside me,
building, rushing into a raging ocean.
When I try to stop it,
when I try to close the floodgates,
I hear her.

This woman inside me screams,
Stop holding me back.
Stop taming me.
Let me go.
You are safe.
Worthy.
Ready.

So, I let her come up.
I feel her.
It's overwhelming at first and then
oh-so-delicious
and powerful.

There's no going back. She
set flame to everything I
once was.

Pour love into yourself
every day.
Don't settle
for   anyone
who does not
match your frequency.

waves rising and falling,
water transforming
bringing life to that which has dried out
swirling, gushing, raging, flowing,
ravishing all that is in her path

feel the sweet nectar,
release your shame and shy
feel it, dear woman,
as it drips down your thighs

What if we all remembered
the way we once walked
through the dark forest
with wild animals beside us,
the way we ran with the wolves
and played with our curiosity,
the way we led with our wisdom
and knew each plant's name?
What if we remembered
that we are the elders,
the witches,
the wild ones
coming back
to claim
what was
always ours?

The stories they tell you
fill up your blood,
and lay within your flesh;
your life, they secretly flood.

They replaced Lilith with Eve,
her noncompliance with submission.
Lilith's story couldn't be told
to an audience in remission.

They made Eve herself
a woman of shame:
her desire to live,
a reason for blame.

The stories—more stories,
too many to tell—
all shaped to hold you
under their spell.

When I step into the world of my heart,
everything changes.
I like it here.

The Universe holds me in her arms,
bats away that which I think I want,
not giving in to my protests.
Hold on, she whispers.
Just wait.

My heart cracks wide open;
my senses are alive.
I trust the process of my vision to thrive.

I receive abundance in all its forms;
I don't deny myself
the beauty of storms.

I am humble and confident in this life I create.
I take full responsibility—
I don't write it off as fate.

It's happening again:
I can feel the cage closing in-—
the one that looks like
square lots
and striped lawns,
blank eyes
and blue screens.
It makes me want to run.

Forest-stained feet,
leaves in my hair,
dirt beneath my nails,
water strips me bare.

I don't fit into the world out there
of small talk and dead smiles,
structured time,
and counting every mile.

My feet are too dirty
for shoes so white;
my spirit, too wild
for a life bound so tight.

Dear woman,
there is a fire inside of your chest
and an ocean between your legs.

They want to make you feel bliss
and ecstasy and heaven,
to create through your life force.

So shed, powerful woman,
every thought and belief,
every feeling that keeps you
from the aliveness of yourself,
from this world.

Break your heart wide open
until you feel as raw and real
as you have ever imagined.

Fight for it—
for the life within you.
Keep going;
we're in this together.
This feeling is our birthright
that's been stripped from us
by a world that was never taught how to hold us.

We've been taught
to be their Mary.

But don't forget
that you are also Lilith.

I suppose these words come
from deep within the well
these sounds I've read and ingested
have made their home within my bones
awoke the wisdom in my heart
created feelings that dance
inside my body
draw images and
spark memories

these words all weave together like a web
a story that wants to be told
they move through my flesh
until I let them borrow my voice
to float on the wave
through the space that moves them
into another
so that it may have their way with them
moving through their flesh
arousing their curiosity
weaving together
stories held by the great mother

your story is mine
and mine yours
for as soon as it is told
is it not absorbed into our very cells?

we all have something to tell
our story is made up of stories
made up of all these words
in the well

You didn't come here to hide in the shadows;
you came here with your light,
your truth.
You came here with songs,
dreams,
fierceness,
fire,
and love.

Stop waiting for permission.
How do you want to live
this one short and wild life—
with your eyes closed
or with your magic?

82

Put me in a bookstore
instead of a bar.
I prefer to lose myself in words
rather than in drink.

We all walk around
with no idea
of how much magic
we hold.

The time will come
when we leave these physical bodies,
when we don't feel anymore:
the sun, the wind,
our hearts beating through our chests,
our children's hands in ours,
our lovers' lips on our skin,
our rage and sadness,
the full spectrum of human emotion.

What a gift to be here,
able to feel how magical
and courageously tender
we are.

I woke to the overflowing laundry basket
of emotions waiting for me
to run them through the wash
or show them the door.
The worn jeans of Resistance were first;
they didn't want to go,
but I stayed strong and let them have
one last day on the couch before leaving.
Judgment was next, a little black dress,
I wore him tight. He clung to every curve,
and I clung back before I unzipped him.
Guilt was up—the sweater my mom got me
that never fit quite right.
I felt bad for letting him go.
I took off my rose-colored glasses of Perception;
the lenses were too foggy with conditioning.
I showered off my lotions of Unworthiness,
watched them swirl down the drain.
My lacy bra of Eagerness went in the trash with
my panty hose of Instant Gratification and
sequined dress of Distractions.
I sat down on the cool grass,
feeling the sun on my face.
I took a deep breath
and allowed myself to be naked.

86

children's laughter
a lover's touch
pen on paper
feet on the earth
a sister's embrace
a garden of blessings

I can't keep up with the world's pace.
My feelings dissipate;
my softness petrifies;
my connections fade;
my magic retreats;
my spirit breaks,
and I can't breathe.

They've burned us at the stake,
violated our wombs,
silenced us with shame and guilt,
and beat us with judgment and fear.

They have tried, dear woman,
for generations to disconnect
us from ourselves.

They have welded the bars
of the cage they put us in,
fearful that we will see past them,
that we will hear the whisper of our hearts
and heed our intuition,
that we will embody the wisdom in our bones
and the wildness in our flesh.

They fear the day you'll remember
that your heart alchemizes their bloodshed,
that your compassion can heal the world.

They fear you, dear woman,
your rise from the ashes.
So, they keep adding their bars.
They fear, dear woman,
that you will remember
who you are.

Maybe the only love affair
we should aim to have
is the one with our own lives.
Maybe we should slow down
and make love with our presence,
embrace everything with softness
and curiosity, allow the world
to penetrate us to our depths
and transform us into our highest potential.
This may be the greatest love affair
of all time.

Give me sunshine,
a pen, paper, and the earth
beneath my body,
and I'll tell you
about all the magic
this world holds.

What might it feel like
to dance with life?

Would it feel like
taking your hair out of an elastic?
Letting your worries fall with each strand?
Putting on the loud music
that courses through your blood?
Circling your hips and arousing your secrets?
Shaking and shimmying years of stagnation
out of your muscles?
Throwing your hair around?

How do you let the world know
you are still alive?

Why be normal
when I can be both
fierce and soft,
loud and quiet,
cosmic and earthly,
fire and rain?
When I can play on the topsoil
and dance in the underworld?
Normal doesn't suit me well;

I am magic.

I would rather wake to a life of full potential
than to sleep in a bed of known tomorrows.

There is an altar inside my heart
that I visit daily.

It's made of crystal and
smells of oils and incense.

I place candles and flowers on it
and clean it often.

I honor this space
and bring all of my struggles and fears to it.

She knows what to do with them.
She wraps them in compassion and love;

they melt and transform
before her beauty.

I devote myself to this space,
this altar inside of my heart.

How tragic it would be to die
without ever meeting yourself.

97

98

Earth

She'll let you walk gently on her ground,
let you come back home to her wisdom.
She'll wrap you in her loving arms,
feed you sweet nectar from her flowers,
and let you drink from her streams—
but don't think it'll be easy.
For once you step into her powerful embrace,
your long-awaited transformation
will take place.

I wonder what the fairies think
of us, stomping around, heads down
as though we've forgotten
all the beauty around us,
as we swat them away annoyed.

Do they wonder when we'll remember
how to tread lightly?

If we can feel the breeze,
the sun, the grass? And, if we can,
why aren't we basking in the magic of it all?

Such strange creatures
they must think of us,
almost as if
we are not real
at all.

The sun never dims his light
for those not ready to see it.
The ocean never wonders
if her depth will be accepted.
The moon moves
through her phases
unapologetically.

-carry on

She is nature
wrapped in flesh;
the cosmos shine
through her eyes.

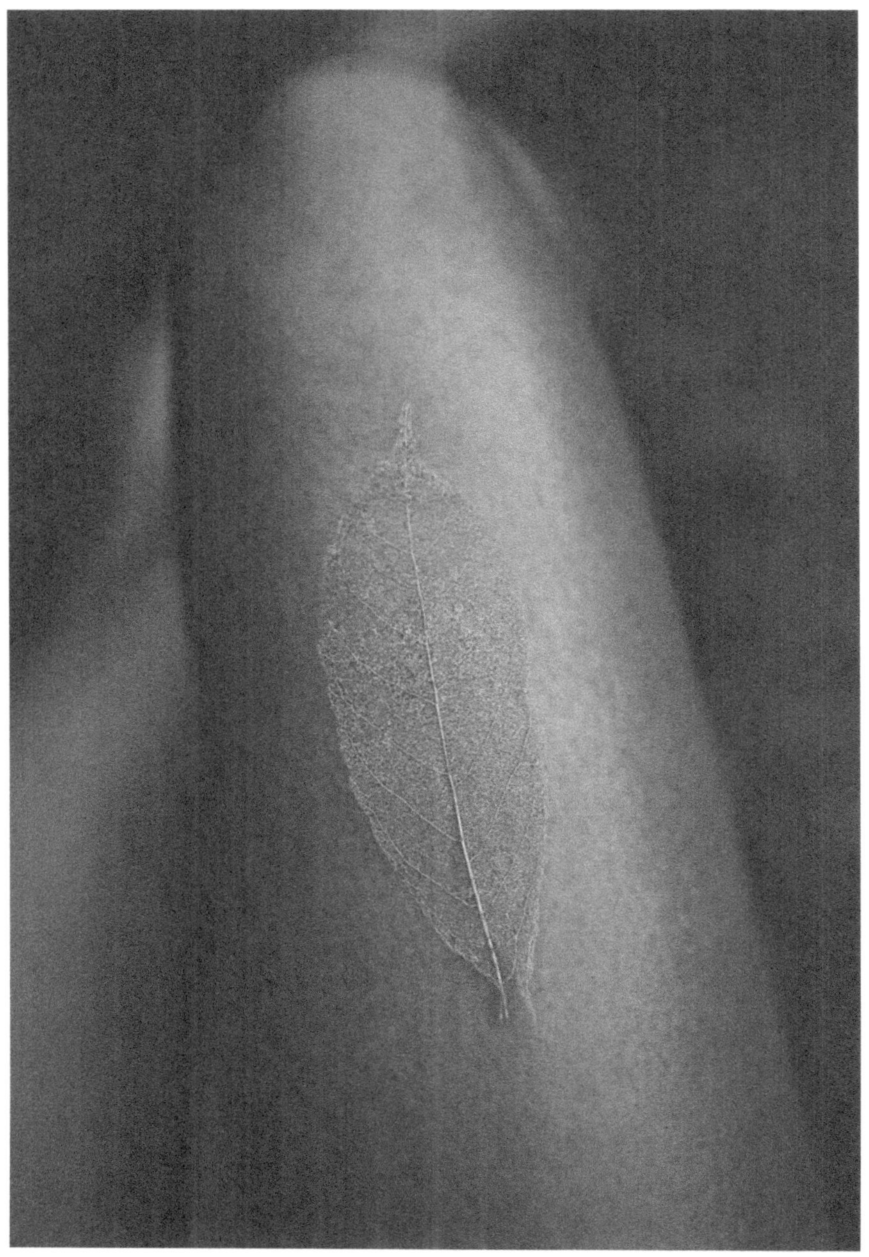

These trees helped me find my voice.
At first the words were a tangled mess,
were drowned out by tears.
Then they turned angry,
hit the leaves with their fight,
until they found notes of love
that swam up from my heart
and onto their bark.
I talked and talked until I was empty,
and finally they asked
how it felt to have a voice.

When you need love,
walk outside and welcome him,
squint at his light,
and unwrap your petals.
You'll feel him
ask, *Will you let me love you?*
You will let your garments
fall to the ground,
let yourself melt into the earth—
let her hold you—
as he claims you.
You will fully surrender
as he penetrates you,
lights up your soul,
turns your yearning
into fulfillment.
He will nourish you,
honor you,
remind you
of the goddess you are.
and you will remember his touch,
his love,
his presence

-the sun

108

May I bloom with the trees this year,
with the wildflowers I know by name.
May I bloom into the next version of myself,
after the many deaths this cold winter has gifted me.

I sit down before her
having dreamt of her
washing away my old skin.
She rises to meet me
as though she has been waiting
for me
just the same.

Waiting to heal,
waiting for a lover,
waiting to feel,
waiting for the right time,
waiting for the next reel.

I wonder if the earth waits
until every blade of grass is even,
for the ocean to stop waving,
for the clouds to disappear.
I wonder if the earth waits
before she decides to live.

Sometimes I sing with the birds
and dance with the trees.
Sometimes I fear, like the deer
running from the wolf.
Sometimes I am the wolf
howling at the moon.
Mostly I am the wildflower
blooming, dying
blooming again—
always

wild and fre!

Isn't it beautiful,
the way the grass holds the dew?
The way he uses all his strength to hold her up
so that the light shines through her,
exposing her fullness,
knowing that his time with her
could never be long enough?

116

Every morning,
when I walk out of the woods,
I walk having remembered
a little bit more
of myself.

The rose opens its petals
every day for the sun,
showing herself fully,
standing tall in her thorns,
and never punishing the darkness that comes,
She is trusting and open
in full surrender.
I wish to be more like her.

We open the door and rush into the car,
not noticing the breeze
that kissed our bodies
or the sun embracing us with his warmth.

We walk by the tree, not recognizing
her endless whispers and offerings.

We hide in our homes, away from the stars
that come out every night to remind us
how to shine in the darkness.

We look upon water as though it's not holy,
able to wash away our heaviness.

Oh, how we have forgotten
the magic of this world,
but she has not forgotten us.

Slow down, she pleads as he speeds by.
Slow down, she offers as he rushes to work.
Slow down, she soothes as his body begins to hurt.
Slow down, she whispers as he masks the pain.
Slow down, she hums when he turns to the bottle.
Slow down, she invites as his body protests.
Let me hold you, she says as his body is placed in
the ground.

123

my hand on the bark of her trunk
the sun dancing on us
the branch playing with her shadow

-and we're told that magic isn't real

I whispered to the earth,
thank you for showing me your magic.

She whispered back,
thank you for looking.

The rain kissed me today;
she fell upon my cheek
as though she had been waiting too long.
I stood there, head back, receiving—
drenched in her,
and instantly transformed.

The sun wraps me in his essence,
warming every part of me,
filling my cells with his love.
The wind gently kisses my skin,
dances with my hair and awakens my breasts,
reminding me to play, to touch.
The water invites me into her depths,
asking me to expose my own,   reminding
me that my wetness is sacred. Today I
feel it all:
how connected we are,
how delicious this life is.

Leave me to the woods
while I dance to her music.

129

It's funny
how we always think
we have to *fix* everything:
leaves on a lawn,
grass that's getting too long,
a woman's anger,
her curious nature.

Our earth holds the stories
of priestesses and well maidens,
river women and goddesses.
Her whispers grow louder;
we can hear them through our hearts.
The elders surround us with sweet songs.
It's time, they say.
It's time to remember.

I bathe in the wild sea
and sip the moonlight.
I dance with the fire
and stand tall with the oak tree.
I am a woman,
deliciously whole,
grounding into this earth
that which flows from the cosmos,
flying with the fairies,
flirting with the gnomes,
howling with the wolves,
or sitting in your arms—
sometimes soft
sometimes a storm.

I left my house needing to go to her,
to sit with the restlessness inside of my body.
I find myself at the ocean;
she is raging,
pounding the earth with her power,
spraying all who stand in front of her.
We sit together,
her and I,
my restlessness
turning into

belonging.

Have you seen the way the sun shines
off the snowflakes?
It's as if he couldn't bear
the thought of her existing
without all of her colors.

The flower doesn't force herself to bloom in the
winter.
She does not try to fight the weight of the snow;
she rests in the darkness
knowing that
the sun will fill her
when the time is right,
and, with ease and grace,
she will rise
and bloom anew.

It scared me
when they sprayed her to stop her growth,
when they fenced in her wild.

It scared me
when they slashed her forests
and dirtied her waters.

It scared me
into silence,
into hiding.

But I watch her
as she grows over the roads she's not allowed,
as her beauty shoots up from that field they plowed.

I watch her
flowers intertwine
with the fence they staked,

I watch her
as she tells you
her wild is not yours to take.

I belong
to the sky,
to the ocean,
to the trees,
to the hawk that flies over head,
to the dragonfly by the river,
to my unruly hair, to
my browned skin,
and to the dirt on my feet.

I feel each movement,
each breath,
each sensation,
as if it were my own
as if we are the same.

What if birdsong
awoke something deep within us?
What if our words were spells
that created our reality?
What if these trees pushed air into our lungs?
What if every interaction is an exchange of energy?
What if sex was sacred?
What if the sun heals and the earth grounds us?
How then, might we walk with all this

magic?

Love

Love me *free*.

144

I was looking for his passion;
he was looking for my settle.
We never met them.

Maybe this next part of my life is about me.

Maybe it's about living more fully in my body,
feeling every moment,
massaging every tense muscle.

Maybe it's about wild self-exploration
and delicious self-pleasure.

Maybe it's about laying on a hammock,
writing poetry, and rocking myself
while the trees dance over me,
and the sun shines His love on me.

Maybe it's about taking the time
to watch the stars and dance under the moon,
to eat by candlelight and sway to soft music.

Maybe it's about tending to myself,
the way I've tended to everyone else.

Freshly manicured grass
was common in our past.
I asked for ours to be left wild;
he gave me a small space
as though I was a child—
tucked in the back
where no one could see,
like the way he wished
my untamed spirit to be.

Every day I grieve
not being able to spend my days
with the image I made up of you.

I drank him in too quickly,
got drunk on his moonlight,
danced around his fire,
had a taste for his magic,
and gulped it down.

And I woke, hungover,
feeling irresponsible
for allowing myself
to be so careless.

He chose not to dive into his own depths,
so he had no idea how to swim in mine.

Every time I spoke,
he couldn't hear me through his walls.

Every time I offered him pieces of me,
he said I was too much.

Every time I gave him my colors,
he left me for a blue reflection.

Every time he ignored my need to grow,
I wilted a little more.

Every time.

I was more afraid to lose myself
than I was to lose you.

Give me your fingers that move
the hair from my eyes,
your lips that trace
the curve of my thighs.

Give me your courage to walk
through doors of initiations,
your primal passion
for your temptations.

Give me your soul
to hold my light,
your hands to carry
my endless nights.

I open to him
the way a flower opens to the sun,
fully and automatically
as if it is the most natural thing
I have ever done.

I walk into the cabin,
my eyes set on the white porcelain
destined to hold me.

He finds me there, soaking under
rose petals, picks up the flickering
candle on the floor, replacing it with himself.

He opens a poetry book—
the one with words that melt me.

His smooth voice runs through my veins
like a drug I can't be without.

He reads to me while I lay there,
immersed in his love for me,
and lost in my love for him.

I wait for each poem to end,
knowing our lips will meet with each flip
of the page.

Again, and again, he reads and kisses me
until my skin is wrinkly,
the water is cool,
and the world is right again.

I think the way I dream scared him.

I dream in emotions,

sacred sex,
love,
depth,
truth,
magic.

He wasn't ready
for me to close my eyes.

You're not allowed to enter my space
until you clean your own.

Don't place me on a pedestal
and shame me for being human.

Don't give me your perfect
and blame me when I walk away.

Instead, dance in our truth and authenticity.
Let our shadows come out to play.

I need a man to be my rock
but not to weigh down my wings.

Do not let those enter
who will not
leave flowers at your feet,
place rose petals on your heart,
pour honey down your hips.

Do not let them enter,
beautiful sister,
unless they light candles on your altar,
leave love inside your temple.

I sat with you today,
our sun-kissed bottoms on the Earth,
children laughing, and I paused
to breathe it all in—
the calmness,
the acceptance,
the space we held—
when a remembrance came over me
that we are one,
that you are my sister,
that we are walking
each other home.

Love me like the river loves to move,
embrace my fluidity,
and touch me in each new moment.

Love me like the breeze loves the leaves
dance with me,
and kiss every inch of my body.

Love me like the sun loves the wildflowers,
warm me,
and help me grow.

Love me fierce,
love me soft,
love me wild.

165

His safety invited me to let go
and let go I did,
over
and over
and over
again.

I'm excited for the day
we lay on the couch,

you on your back and me on my side,
my arm and leg draped over you,

head resting on your shoulder,
hand on your chest,

feeling the vibration of your voice
move through me,

as you tell me the story
that brought you home to me.

He touched me,
oh, how he touched me.

His presence moved into
the rooms that held my trauma.
A childhood filled with rage,
past lives filled with abuse—
he felt it all. He pressed
his fingers ever-so-gently
until he pushed deeper with intention.
He held me as my body gave way
to him in sweet release,
making more room
for my spirit to enter.

Oh, how he touched me.

Tell me only truths—
nothing more,
nothing less—
for there is no stronger love
than one forged in truth.

I daydream about skinny dipping with him.
Where are you going? he asks,
and I tell him about the full moon
and my need to swim naked under her.

Come with me, I flirt,
and he does.
But then I leave that dream aside
and replace it with a new one.

I go to the sea by myself,
undress and walk into her embrace,
melting into her.

I lay on top of her and stare at the stars,
and an even better feeling fills me—
peace—for having the courage

to do this,
to live.

I had no choice but to trust;
my heart wouldn't listen to me.
It didn't hear the cries of my walls;
it was already in your hands.

You make me be more of me,
what better way to love someone?

I have you, he promised.

I trust you, I replied.

The soft undulation
of his fingers between my thighs
sends waves through my spine.
His eyes locked on mine,
my head drops back,
and I surrender in his hands.

It wasn't his looks
or the way he made me laugh.
It wasn't the way he touched
my back softly and made me melt inside
or his smile that made me blush.
It was his presence—
the way he looked right through me
and made me feel seen
for the first time in my life.
That made my walls collapse
as though they had never existed
at all.

Do we have what it takes to
move through the cycles of
our love,
our   lives,
our selves?

I'm willing to find out.

Let me love you;
let me honor you
and the way you have answered the call
even when you were alone.
The way you walk your dharma
and live with purpose.

Let me acknowledge you
and your commitment
to serve,
your commitment
to your soul,
your growth.

Let me acknowledge
your integrity,
your steadiness,
your safety,
and your love.

Let me honor you;
let me love you.

It was here laying in your arms
feeling the rise and fall of your chest
as you slept
that I apologized to the Universe,
for ever having questioned it.

We were a beautiful mess
of skin and sweat,
rolled into the centers of our hearts,
unsure of whose was whose.

His hands hold integrity
and self-love;
they also hold me.

He does it without my control,
without my understanding.

He carries my body to safety,
a place of such trust

that my walls cave in,
as though they weren't built with cement.

One look makes me crumble,
and by the time he touches me,

I am already undone.

our feet tangle in the bed sheets
your hands tangle in my hair
your tongue tangles with mine

the only thing unraveling
is my heart

he moved with me
slowly
intentionally
not losing himself
as if to say
there is no rush
I'm going to ravish you
in every possible way

one button

at a time

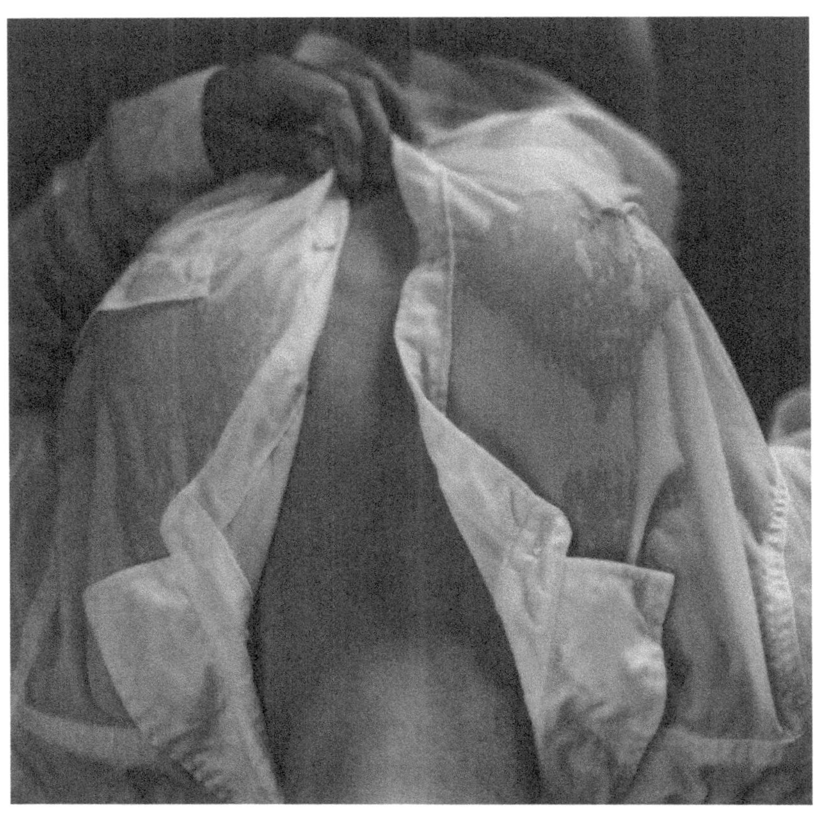

Let him adore you, my love.
You don't have to perform
or be someone you are not.
Let him simply adore you, my love,
for all that you are.

Come, I'm going to make love to you,
he whispered.

You already are,
I whispered back.

I dance often
with my eyes closed,
letting the music move me.
I circle my hips and sway my spine,
make love to my soul.
I ground into my magic,
but I must admit
I enjoy it more
when you are watching me.

He doesn't hold me
with dead arms,
an empty body,
and a wandering mind.

He holds me
with his love,
authenticity,
and undeniable power—

this is how he claims me.

He is the sky
in which she beats her wings.

He is the sky
that makes space for her storms.

He is the sky
that holds all of her.

What if she never feels it?
The shaking of her hips?
The opening of her heart?
The trembling of her legs?
The releasing of her walls?
The shiver up her spine?
The gush of her ocean?
The depth of her body?
The satisfied smirk of a man who's done his work?

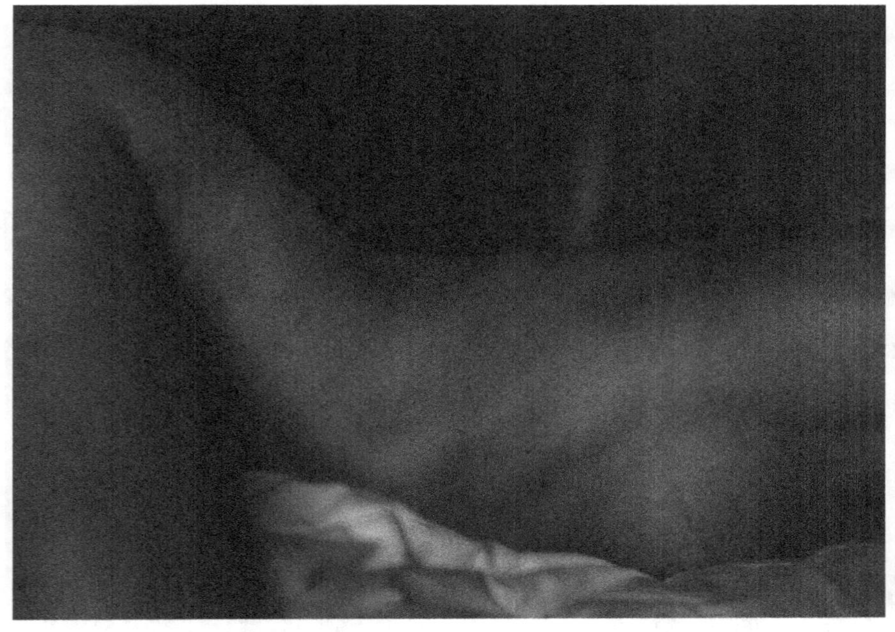

He pressed his lips against mine.
I thought I heard him speak
about all the time
he could spend here,
but I wasn't certain of his whispers— for
he was nowhere near my ears to hear.

He makes love to me
softly, slowly, patiently,
moving with his certainty.
I surrender to his
soft lips and steady hands.
He knows without words
which parts of my body ache for his touch,
as though he can hear my pleas from within—
right here, please right here—
and he answers them,
never faltering in
his devotion,
his service to me.

Sit, my king,
let me dance for you.

He walks into our candle-lit cabin,
drenched from the rain
to find me swaying to the sound
of the guitar dancing with the harmonica.
My hands are in the dried herbs;
their scent fills the room.
I feel him watching me;
his gaze burns through my body,
arousing my womb—
she says yes before I give in.
When I meet his eyes,
the candles jump with excitement,
knowing what comes next.

200

I feel him when he's not with me.
His energy washes over me like a breeze,
wrapping me in love,
touching my skin,
arousing every cell.

It was as though all that was in it for him
was to see me fully open,
to make me feel my own depths,
and to bring me back home to myself.

Can you see her and the tension
in her muscles?
Can you invite them to soften?
Can you see the love in her heart
and protect it with your truth?

Are you so in tune to her
you can feel her breath—
when she holds it
and when she lets go—
when it quickens to ask for more?

Will you honor her?
Pour honey on her womb,
run your fingers down her back,
breathe tenderly on her thighs,
penetrate her with your passion?

Give her your safety,
your hands,
your word.

See her,
honor her.

Can you see him and the commitment
he makes to grow for you?
Can you hold his hands
and appreciate all they provide?
Can you feel his tension
and love him into softness?

Will you honor him?
Open your heart and body to him?
Kiss his neck with your playfulness?
Run your fingers across his thighs?
Worship his firmness in your hands?

Give him your bliss,
your trust,
your love
to wash away
his shadows.

See him,
honor him.

Thank you
xoxo

Connect with Jacquelyn on her Instagram
page
@JacquelynMello

You may also find more of her work on her
website at www.JacquelynMello.com